The Victorians

Written by Theodore Rowland-Entwistle

Illustrated by Sean Duggan

HENDERSON
PUBLISHING PLC

©1994 HENDERSON PUBLISHING PLC

THE VICTORIAN AGE

Queen Victoria's reign began in 1837.
It lasted 63 years, the longest of any
British monarch.

So many changes took place during it that
'the Victorian Age' is used to refer to a
definite period in history. That age actually
lasted for several years after her death. World
War I, which began in 1914, brought a
complete break with the past.

The Young Queen

Victoria was only 18 when she became
queen. Her mother, the Duchess of Kent,
brought her up strictly. As soon as she
became queen, Victoria shook off her
mother's influence. She learned about politics
from her first prime minister, Lord
Melbourne, a Whig.

By the time she died, she was related
through her husband and her children to
most of the crowned heads of Europe.

THE BRITISH EMPIRE

Britain lost its North American colonies in the 1700s. But during the Victorian Age, it built up the largest empire ever known.

British colonial rulers brought European ideas and stable government to many parts of the world. Several parts of the empire became self-governing and independent.

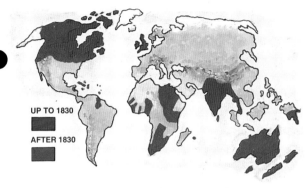

UP TO 1830

AFTER 1830

Many people in the colonies were being exploited. As a result, the British Empire broke up after World War II.

LITTLE WARS

In 1838 the First Afghan War broke out. It was one of many little wars that occurred during the Victorian Age. There were three Afghan wars, fought to restrain Russia from trying to penetrate India through Afghanistan. Later Britain fought Russia in support of Turkey. In Africa there were wars against the Zulus and to defend Egypt. At the end of the 19th century the Dutch Boers (farmers) of South Africa rebelled against British rule.

There was also a rebellion in India.

PHOTOGRAPHY

In **1839** an English scientist, William Henry Fox-Talbot, invented the first method of making photographic paper negatives, and taking positive prints from them.

The use of glass plates instead of paper, resulting in a clearer picture, was invented in 1851 by William Archer, a sculptor.

PRINCE ALBERT

From very early in Victoria's life, her mother, the Duchess of Kent, and the duchess's brother, King Leopold of the Belgians, had a husband planned for her.

He was Prince Albert of Saxe-Coburg-Gotha, Victoria's first cousin on her mother's side. He was a very good-looking young man, serious, conscientious and a lover of music. After some hesitation, Victoria asked him to marry her - as queen, she had to do the proposing. They were married in 1840.

Albert's influence on the queen was enormous. He was strictly moral, and quickly cured Victoria of a tendency to be frivolous.

PENNY POST

Up to 1840 postage on letters was charged by distance as well as weight, and had to be paid by the person receiving them.
In that year Britain introduced uniform rates for letters of the same weight, to be paid for by the sender. Prepayment was made by adhesive stamps.

The system was the idea of a retired schoolmaster, Rowland Hill. He also suggested the use of envelopes, instead of sealing a folded sheet with sealing wax.

The world's first stamps were the Penny Black and Twopenny Blue. They were cancelled in red. In 1841 the penny stamp was changed to red so that black ink could be used for cancellation.

NEW ZEALAND

Also in 1840, Britain annexed New Zealand as a colony. It signed a treaty with the Maori inhabitants called the Treaty of Waitangi.

About 500 Maori chiefs signed the treaty. Within ten years 30,000 Europeans, mostly from Britain, had settled in New Zealand.

FACTORY ACTS

Workers in the Victorian Age found an unexpected champion in Lord Ashley, son of the Earl of Shaftesbury (a title he inherited in 1851).

Ashley was appalled at conditions in factories and mines.

As a result of his campaigning, the Mines Act of 1842 banned women, boys under 10 and girls from working underground.

Two years later the first of two Factory Acts reduced the working day for children between 8 and 13 to 6 hours, and that for women of all ages from 13 upward to 12 hours. In 1847 the working day for women and young persons was reduced to 10 hours.

Brunel Junior surveyed and laid out
the Great Western Railway. He also
built three passenger ships, each
the biggest in the world when it
was launched. The first was
the wooden-hulled paddle-
steamer 'Great Western'.

The second was the 'Great
Britain', the first big iron-
hulled screw-propelled ship.
This ship is now displayed at Bristol.

The third was the 'Great Eastern', for
40 years the world's largest ship. It was not
a commercial success, but it laid the first
successful transatlantic cable in 1866.

THE FIRST CO-OP

Britain's first co-operative society was the Rochdale Society of Equitable Pioneers. It was established in 1844 in Toad Lane (t'Owd [Old] Lane), Rochdale, Lancashire.

Like all modern co-ops it was designed to provide members with good quality food at fair prices.

YMCA and YWCA
The Young Men's Christian Association (YMCA) was founded in London in 1844 to provide a place where young male shop workers could meet and read the Bible. It now has 25 million members worldwide.

The Young Women's Christian Association (YWCA) was formed in 1870.

IRISH FAMINE

In 1845 a blight ruined about three-quarters of Ireland's potato crop, the main food for 4,000,000 people.

Most of Ireland's wheat and other food was exported. The money for it went to absentee landlords.

A second potato failure in 1846 led to a famine that lasted four years. About a million Irish died, and two million emigrated to America. The episode left the Irish with a bitter hatred of Britain.

ELECTRIC TELEGRAPH

The electric telegraph was invented and developed early in the Victorian Age. The first users in Britain were the railways, to control train movements.

The Morse Code, invented by an American artist, Samuel Morse, made transmission and reception of messages easy, and was universally used. The first cable carrying messages between Britain and France was laid in 1851.

Pneumatic Tyre

The world's first pneumatic tyre was invented by a Scottish engineer, Robert William Thomson, in 1845. But it was expensive to make and hard to fit and remove, and the idea was soon forgotten.

The tyre was re-invented in 1888 by John Boyd Dunlop, a Belfast veterinary surgeon. His tyre could be removed easily. Pneumatic tyres were soon used by all cyclists, and every car was fitted with them by the early 1900s.

NEW IDEAS

In 1849 Mrs. Elizabeth Jesser Reid founded a college for the higher education of women. At that time few women had a chance to progress beyond high school.

It was named Bedford College, because it was first based at Bedford Square, in London. It was one of the first colleges to train women for social work.

It is now part of Royal Holloway and Bedford New College, in the University of London.

Chloroform

Sir James Simpson, professor of midwifery at the University of Edinburgh, introduced the use of chloroform to lessen the pain of childbirth in 1847.

Some Church leaders thought it was wrong for women to be spared pain in this way, but they stopped objecting when Queen Victoria had it for the birth of her eighth child, Prince Leopold, in 1853.

DISEASE HITS LONDON

The disease of cholera came to Britain in 1831. There were several outbreaks, especially on Tyneside. In 1849 a major epidemic hit London. It was worst in an area around Golden Square, Soho, where 500 people died in ten days.

Dr. John Snow, Queen Victoria's obstetrician, investigated, and discovered that most of the deaths were among people who drank water from a pump in Broad Street (now Broadwick Street).

Asked what was to be done, he replied: 'Take the handle off the Broad Street pump.' This was done, and the outbreak died down.

Water Supplies

Snow proved that cholera was a water-borne disease. Some water supplies (including the well under the Broad Street pump) were being contaminated by leaking sewage.

Water supplies were inadequate in London. In some areas the water was turned on for only a few hours a day. Much of the water was drawn from the polluted River Thames.

The supply problem was not solved until early in the 1900s.

THE GREAT STINK

In the hot summer of 1858 a dreadful smell pervaded London. It became known as the Great Stink.

The cause of the stink was the River Thames. The sewers poured raw sewage into it all the time. Joseph Bazalgette, chief engineer to the Metropolitan Board of Sewers, solved the problem by building a new system of sewers. It carried the waste to a treatment plant east of London. These sewers are still in use today.

PUBLIC TRANSPORT

Horse-drawn buses first appeared in Britain in 1829. The first double-decker bus ran in London in 1851. The first petrol bus was introduced in 1905.

Longer road journeys were by stage coach, but the railways replaced most of the stage coach services by the mid 1800s.

Queen Victoria helped the spread of railways by using trains herself, which overcame many people's objections to them - and their fears.

AT THE SAME TIME

Because trains had to keep to a timetable, railways had the effect of standardising time throughout the country.

Before that, the time shown on public clocks varied from place to place.

Mixing

Before the railway age, many people never travelled far from their homes. Some, indeed, barely knew their next village.

One result of railways was that people did not have to live within walking distance of their work. They could move out to cleaner suburbs around the big towns.

THE GREAT EXHIBITION

In 1851 the world's first international exhibition was held in London. The idea for the Great Exhibition was first mooted in 1850, and was eagerly followed up by Prince Albert, who oversaw the planning of it.

A huge hall of cast iron and glass was erected in Hyde Park. Londoners promptly called it the Crystal Palace. There were more than 13,000 exhibitors, from all over the world.

Queen Victoria was worried over the large number of birds in the hall, which threatened to damage exhibits. The aged Duke of Wellington advised her: 'Try sparrowhawks, Ma'am.'

The Crystal Palace was later moved to Sydenham in south London. It was destroyed by fire in 1936.

CRIMEAN WAR

In 1854 Britain and France went to war against Russia in support of the Ottoman Empire in Turkey. The conflict lasted until 1856.

The causes of the war included the Muslim Turks' harsh treatment of Christians, and Russia's need for access for its warships through the Turkish-controlled Dardanelles Strait. Russia threatened Turkey's shipping and its Black Sea coast.

Fighting took place in the Crimea, a Black Sea peninsula, now part of Ukraine. The war was the first big conflict covered by newspaper reporters and photographers.

FLORENCE NIGHTINGALE

The worst feature of the Crimean War was the lack of medical care. Soldiers were dying like flies from wounds and disease. Florence Nightingale, a society lady who had taken up nursing - to the horror of her family - was sent out with 38 nurses to take control. She saved hundreds of lives.

When the war ended she returned to England, her own health severely damaged. She campaigned to reform all army hospital care, and also health care in England.

EXPLORATION OF AFRICA

Britain's influence in Africa was greatly strengthened by the travels of David Livingstone, a Scottish missionary doctor.

Livingstone explored the Zambesi River and several lakes. He gave the Victoria Falls their English name (the local name was Mosi oa Tunya, the Smoke that Thunders). In a book he exposed the activities of Arab slave traders in eastern Africa.

Other British explorers in Africa included Sir Richard Burton and John Hanning Speke in East Africa; Sir Henry Stanley in Zaire; and Mungo Park in the Niger River basin.

A NEW PALACE

The year Queen Victoria came to the throne work began on rebuilding the Houses of Parliament, destroyed by fire in 1834. The new Palace of Westminster was completed in 1860.

One of the finishing touches was the installation of the clock and its famous bell, Big Ben.

ATTITUDES CHANGE

Before 1858 nobody in England and Wales could obtain a divorce except by a private Act of Parliament, costing many hundreds of pounds. In that year a new divorce court was set up. In Scotland divorce had been possible since 1560.

Evolution

A sensation was caused in 1858 when the naturalist Charles Darwin published his book 'On the Origin of Species', in which he set out the theory of evolution.

His views were supported by his fellow scientist, Alfred Russel Wallace. But religious leaders denounced the theory as contrary to the teachings of the Bible.

DEATH OF ALBERT

The Prince Consort was already ill with typhoid fever when he intervened in the 'Trent' affair. Fourteen days later he was dead.

Queen Victoria had lost her most valuable adviser, who had shared with her the burden of the throne. Her grief was overwhelming, and for twenty years she withdrew as much as possible from public life. This made her less popular with the general public. However, she kept a watchful eye on the activities of her ministers.

BUSY MRS. BEETON

A remarkable book appeared in 1861 that has been a best-seller ever since: 'Mrs. Beeton's Household Management'. It was written by Mrs. Isabella Beeton, a 25 year old housewife.

The book covered everything a housewife ought to know. Recipes ranged from elaborate dinners for 18 persons to an economical soup at 3d (just over 1p) a quart.

Mrs. Beeton advised that a household with an income of £1,000 a year should expect to have a staff of five: cook, upper housemaid, nursemaid, under housemaid and a man servant.

SPORT

The Football Association was formed in 1863, but football was still mainly a school sport until the 1870s. The first FA Cup competition was held in the winter of 1871-1872. The Football League was formed in 1888-1889.

In 1862 an English cricket team visited Australia for the first time. In 1866 the Marquess of Queensberry's rules for boxing were adopted.

Spharistiké

A new game was introduced in 1874 by Major Walter Wingfield. He called it Spharistiké. It was based on the ancient game now called Royal Tennis. Because it was played on lawns it became known as lawn tennis.

The first All-England Championship was held at Wimbledon in 1877.

DISRAELI AND GLADSTONE

Two remarkable men dominated British politics between 1868 and 1894. They were Benjamin Disraeli and William Gladstone.

Benjamin Disraeli was leader of the Conservatives. He was the first Jew to become prime minister, a post he held briefly in 1868, and from 1874 to 1880. He was a novelist, a dandy, and somewhat flamboyant. His health was not strong. But his exotic good looks concealed great patriotism and political skill. Queen Victoria liked him very much.

Gladstone

William Gladstone, the Liberal leader, was prime minister four times: 1868-1874, 1880-1885, 1886 and 1892-1894. He combined good health and vigour with devotion to duty.

Gladstone was a great administrator. He favoured Home Rule for Ireland, and introduced a Reform Act which almost doubled the number of men eligible to vote in Britain. Queen Victoria detested him.

UNDERGROUND!

The world's first underground railway opened in 1863. It was the Metropolitan Line in London. It ran from Paddington Station to Farringdon Street Station. It was built on the cut-and-cover principle, running mostly under main roads. There was one tunnel. By 1884 it had been extended, and made a complete circuit of central London (the present Circle Line). At first the trains were hauled by steam locomotives, but electric trains were introduced later. The first deep-level 'Tube' was opened in 1890.

NEW HOUSING

The jerry-built houses of the Industrial Revolution created many slums in Britain's towns. Their replacement by decent housing was partly due to the efforts of a reformer, Octavia Hill.

From 1864 onward she bought up slum property to improve or replace it.

In 1895 she became one of the founders of the National Trust.

CHIMNEY SWEEPS

One of the scandals of the 19th century was the use of small boys to climb up chimneys to sweep them.

It was brought to the public's notice by a clergyman, novelist and history professor, Charles Kingsley. He wrote a fairy tale about a chimney sweep, 'The Water Babies', which was published in 1863. Parliament passed two Bills outlawing the practice, in 1863 and 1875.

THE ALICE BOOKS

One of the most popular children's books ever, 'Alice's Adventures in Wonderland', was published in 1865.
It was written by a mathematics lecturer at the University of Oxford, Charles Dodgson. He used the pen-name of Lewis Carroll. He followed it in 1871 with 'Through the Looking Glass'. Queen Victoria loved the stories and asked for a copy of his next book. To her disappointment it was a learned book on mathematics.

Dr. Barnado's

Dr. Barnardo's Homes for destitute children were founded by an Irish clerk, Thomas

Barnado, who went to London to study medicine. Barnardo was so appalled at the plight of homeless orphans that he opened a mission, and his first home, while he was still studying medicine.

The Trades Union Congress was founded in 1868 by a group of unions anxious about their legal status.

The TUC worked to secure new laws about trade unions, and to find a way of having workers' views represented in Parliament. As a result trade unions were formally declared legal in 1871.

A separate Scottish TUC was formed in 1897.

Legal Reforms

A number of reforms in the legal system were carried through in the late 1800s. The punishment of transportation - sending convicts to penal settlements abroad - came to an end in 1868.

In 1869 imprisonment for debt was abolished.

EDUCATION

Compulsory elementary education for all children came in between 1870 and 1880.

The first step was to give local authorities power to provide elementary schools.

As soon as the schools were available, a further law made it compulsory for every child to go to school, and fees in State schools were abolished.

Home Rule

Many Irishmen demanded home rule for their country. The Home Rule Association, which called for an Irish parliament to deal with domestic affairs, was set up in 1870. Protestants in Northern Ireland opposed the idea.

William Gladstone made two attempts to get a Home Rule Bill through Parliament. The first was defeated in the Commons, the second in the Lords. Home Rule was not achieved until after World War I (1914-1918).

BUYING A CANAL

The Suez Canal was built by the French and the Turkish rulers of Egypt, and opened in 1869. In 1875 the bankrupt ruler of Egypt offered his shares in the canal company to Britain.

Disraeli, the prime minister, accepted. In order to act quickly, he borrowed the money from the international bankers Rothschilds until Parliament could confirm the deal.

The Telephone

Alexander Graham Bell, a Scottish emigrant to the United States, invented the telephone in 1876. Within three years the first British telephone exchange opened in London, with ten subscribers.

TUNNEL VISION

Britain and France agreed to dig a tunnel under the English Channel in 1876. Experimental tunnels were bored from both sides.

Disputes between rival railway companies in England led the matter to be referred to a committee of the House of Commons. The committee voted 6-4 against the tunnel, and work stopped in 1882.

English Channel

More Voters

A third Reform Act was passed in 1884. It made 2,000,000 more men eligible to vote, leaving only domestic servants, bachelors living at home, and men with no fixed abode voteless.

At the same time constituencies were reorganized to make them of roughly equal size.

POLLI BOOTH T to Z

TWO JUBILEES

Queen Victoria celebrated her Golden Jubilee in 1887. A Thanksgiving service was held in Westminster Abbey, at which music by Prince Albert was performed.  The queen was astonished at her popularity and the celebrations. But she refused to wear her robes of state. Instead of the crown she wore a bonnet, trimmed with lace and diamonds. Much greater celebrations marked her Diamond Jubilee ten years later. London streets were decorated, the new electric light adding to the brilliance of the display.

County Councils

Local government was transformed in 1888 with the creation of 62 county councils. Each county had one, and some of the larger ones, such as Yorkshire, had more. London was also made a county.

For the first time women got a vote. If they were householders they could vote in elections for the new councils.

Match Girls Strike

Unskilled workers were becoming more militant. In 1888 the women and girls working at a match factory in London went on strike for better pay and conditions.

Their wages were low, and they had to work with the dangerous chemical phosphorous. This caused a terrible disease which affected their teeth and jaw bones.

They won the day, with the support of Annie Besant, editor of 'The Link', a socialist newspaper. Other women workers also won better pay and conditions by striking that year.

For some time trade unionists had wanted representation in Parliament. The first step toward this was taken by a Scottish miner, James Keir Hardie.

In 1888 he founded the Scottish Parliamentary Labour Party. In the general election of 1892, Hardie and two other trade union leaders were elected to Parliament, standing as independents.

The following year an Independent Labour Party was formed in England.

ON THE ROAD

Horse-drawn trams were in use in Britain from the 1860s. In 1891 Leeds installed Britain's first electric tramway system.

The first petrol-driven cars were made in Germany in the 1880s. Britain built its first cars in 1895, and the first motor buses were on London's streets in 1905.

Red Flag Days

When steam traction engines came on to Britain's roads an Act was passed requiring a man to walk well ahead of any mechanical vehicle with a red flag, to warn people it was coming.

Speed was limited to 2 miles an hour in towns and 4 miles an hour in the country. This held back car development in Britain until it was repealed in 1896.

THE WIRELESS

Radio was invented in 1894 by Guglielmo Marconi, a 20-year-old Italian. He could get no financial backing in Italy, so he moved to Britain.

'The wireless', as radio was called for many years, developed rapidly. In 1901 Marconi sent the first message across the Atlantic Ocean.

For several years all transmissions were in morse code, but they enabled ships at sea to keep in touch with land.

SUFFRAGETTES

Women's suffrage - votes for women - became an active campaign in 1897. Millicent Fawcett, sister of the pioneer woman doctor, Elizabeth Garrett Anderson, founded the National Union of Women's Suffrage Societies (NUWSS).

The NUWSS believed in working for its cause by peaceful means. Many women were impatient. In 1903 Emmeline Pankhurst and her daughters, Sylvia and Christabel, formed a militant group, the Women's Social and Political Union (WSPU).

Over the next 11 years WSPU members used increasingly violent tactics to forward their cause. They chained themselves to railings and smashed windows. They fought running battles with police, in which many were injured and two were killed.

Many suffragettes, as they were called, were put in prison. There they went on hunger strike, and were brutally force-fed.

MOVING PICTURES

The first moving picture seen in London showed a London shoeblack in action. It was shown at Finsbury Technical College in 1896.

Public showings of films followed a few weeks later. Soon eight different theatres were showing films.

VICTORIA DIES

Queen Victoria died on January 22, 1901, aged 81. Her people felt it was the end of an era. Many had never known any other ruler.

But although great changes were taking place, most of the Victorian way of life was to continue until the eve of World War I in 1914.

Edward VII

Edward VII was 60 when he became king. His mother had never allowed him to take any part in the business of the monarchy. He was such a complete contrast to his austere and competent father.

Edward was affable, a dandy and a sportsman. Deprived of a real job, he spent much of his time in a busy social life. He was happily married, but had Lillie Langtry, an actress, as his mistress.

ROYAL DIPLOMAT

Edward's happy-go-lucky exterior concealed a shrewd brain. He knew the other crowned heads of Europe (most of them were his relations), and had already acted as a kind of unofficial diplomat. He spoke fluent French and German.

He had to exercise his diplomatic powers to the full during his short reign, especially on his ambitious nephew, Kaiser Wilhelm II of Germany.

Edward did his best to avert World War I, towards which Europe was moving.

Entente Cordiale

Fearing the rapidly growing armed might of Germany, Britain and France signed an 'Entente Cordiale' (Friendly Agreement) in 1904. Russia later joined the pact, and it became known as the 'Triple Entente'.

Edward VII's diplomacy helped the signing of these two treaties.

NEW SPEED LIMIT

A new speed limit of 20 mph (32 km/h) was introduced in 1903. Many magistrates and local police forces enforced it rigorously, setting speed traps to catch motorists.

Two years later a group of motorists founded the Automobile Association (AA) to combat this persecution. The AA patrolmen rode around on motorcycles. They saluted every car bearing an AA badge. If a patrolman failed to salute, the motorist would stop - apparently to rebuke him, but actually to be warned of a speed trap ahead.

BOY SCOUTS

One of the heroes of the Boer War, in South Africa was Major-General Robert Baden-Powell, who helped successfully defend Mafeking whilst it was besieged by the Dutch Boer troops.

Baden-Powell thought boys needed more outdoor life than they could get in school. In 1907 he started the Boy Scout movement. The Girl Guides movement was started two years later.

A NEW KING

When Edward VII died, he was universally mourned. He was succeeded by his son, George V.

The new king was a quiet and dignified man. He not only faced a constitutional crisis, but was to head his country through its worst war so far.

In 1911 Parliament changed the constitution. It reduced the period between general elections from seven years to five; banned the House of Lords from vetoing money Bills; and provided that any Bill, if rejected by the Lords, should become law if passed three times by the Commons.

This marked a major break with the tradition of the Victorian Age, which had already passed into history.